AF590011

IMMORTAL EYE
GOD THEORY: SECOND EDITION

God's View of Man
Man's View of God
Hawking vs. God
Predestination, Evolution
The ORIGIN of Everything

Stephen Blaha Ph. D.
Blaha Research

Ex Scienta In Sapientia
Blaha

Pingree-Hill Publishing
MMXVIII

ISBN: 978-1-7328245-0-8

Cover: The cover depicts the "immortal eye" as a symbolic representation of God from William Blake's poem *The Tyger*. It also shows prehistoric cave drawings of horses from Spain with spirals superimposed. Such spirals have often been seen in prehistoric cave drawings.

Rev. 00/00/01 October 23, 2018

To My Grandchildren:

Milan, Maxim, Alexandre, and Nicholas

How happy is he born and taught,
That serveth not another's will;
Whose armor is his honest thought,
And simple truth his utmost skill!
The Character of a Happy Life,
Sir Henry Wotton (1568-1639)

Some Other Books by Stephen Blaha

All the Megaverse! Starships Exploring the Endless Universes of the Cosmos using the Baryonic Force (Blaha Research, Auburn, NH, 2014)

SuperCivilizations: Civilizations as Superorganisms (McMann-Fisher Publishing, Auburn, NH, 2010)

All the Universe! Faster Than Light Tachyon Quark Starships & Particle Accelerators with the LHC as a Prototype Starship Drive Scientific Edition (Pingree-Hill Publishing, Auburn, NH, 2011).

The Unified SuperStandard Model and the Megaverse SECOND EDITION A Deeper Theory based on a New Particle Functional Space that Explicates Quantum Entanglement Spookiness (Pingree Hill Publishing, Auburn, NH, 2018).

Cosmos Creation: The Unified SuperStandard Model, Volume 2, SECOND EDITION (Pingree Hill Publishing, Auburn, NH, 2018).

Available on Amazon.com, bn.com Amazon.co.uk and other international web sites as well as at better bookstores (through Ingram Distributors).

CONTENTS

FIGURES and TABLES

INTRODUCTION

Most people on earth believe in a God of some form. In this book we will assume that God exists. We will address questions about God and the Cosmos (all of Creation) that can be answered by Logic and Scientific Analysis. We will see that surprising insights follow from this quest for knowledge of God and the Cosmos. A comparison of our findings with the descriptions of God and Creation in major religions shows a remarkable number of similarities. We leave it to the Readers to make of it what they will.

This Second Edition of God Theory contains the material of the First Edition, expanded to include a wider view of God and Creation. In particular we add a discussion of Creationism vs. Evolution and show that Evolution is favored because God clearly shows that God's Laws of Physics are not violated. Whereas the direct creation of Mankind, depicted in religious writings, clearly violates Physical Laws and their consequent Biological Laws. The "morality" of Evolution and "Survival of the Fittest" is considered.

We also show that there is a "Tape of Fate" that contains all history in all detail for all time: past, present and future. God is fully aware of the entire tape at all times. Yet God can perform miracles and change history using Quantum "tweaks." Paradoxically God is aware, at all times, of the tweaks that he has made or will make.

God is also shown to be the ultimate Quantum Observer eliminating Quantum paradoxes and answering questions such as "Is there a sound if no one is there to listen?"

While God Theory is about Mankind's view of God we also consider God's view of Mankind and its possibly "unsettling" consequences.

We were led to this study of God from a scientific view by the development of a fundamental Theory of Everything, The Unified SuperStandard Model, that we derived from a relatively simple set of axioms. The set of axioms led to a derivation of The Unified SuperStandard Model that unifies all matter and their forces in a direct manner. The derivation is presented in volumes 1 and 2 of the Second Edition of *The Unified*

SuperStandard Model and the Megaverse. It is not necessary to be familiar with these books except to realize these volumes provide a derivation of a Theory of Everything from basic axioms in the manner of Euclid's derivation of Geometry. Their beginning point was a "supposed" entity that follows certain "simple" rules to define the axioms governing the Cosmos and thereby leads to the derivation of the physical Cosmos. (The Cosmos consists of the entirety of Creation.)

A remarkable aspect of the "entity" is its similarity to features that most people attribute to God. This book makes a "leap of faith" and assumes the Entity is God. We then take the universally agreed fundamental features of God and proceed to investigate the physical side of God's nature.

In a sense we have joined Physics and Theology.

Some remarkable results follow: 1) God needs the Cosmos; 2) the Cosmos exists forever into the past and the future; 3) the Godhead consists of at least three parts: the Unmoved Mover, the Cosmos, and the Connection between them—functionally a triune God; 4)The Cosmos and Connection parts of God have a God-like spark that is present in the particles of the Unified SuperStandard Model (or perhaps a similar Theory of Everything); 5) Predestination and Free Will are made consistent by the Quantum nature of the Cosmos and the Connection.

The eternal natures of the Cosmos and the Connection have important implications for Physics. In particular, they may require an infinite chain of aeons of universes in which our universe is but one link in the chain. They are consistent with a Megaverse containing universes strewn through a higher dimensional space, much like galaxies are strewn throughout our universe.

Mankind's View of God

1. Generally Assumed Attributes of God

The nature of God has many different forms in the world's religions. However all known religions[1] have a primal God that begins it all. Some religions then proceed to have the first god create further gods. We will assume there is only one God in this book letting beings created with God-like features be viewed as "spirits" that may or may not have certain God-like powers.

In this chapter we will summarize the generally accepted "features" of God.

1.1 Properties of God

God is generally viewed as having certain central powers and properties:

1. Omniscience – God knows all—past, present, and future.

2. Omnipotence – God is all powerful with unlimited abilities.

3. Omnipresence – God is everywhere at all times.

God is often called the *Unmoved Mover* meaning that He is unchanging but causes all events in the Cosmos to happen.

Some further features of God are

1. God has no size. But He cannot be considered to exist as a mathematical "point" either.

[1] Some would this "coincidence" as evidence of knowledge infused in Man by God.

2. God consists of "pure spirit", an incorporeal entity. We take spirit to mean not consisting of matter or energy—yet existant.[2]

3. God has always existed and will always exist.

4. God wants prayer and sacrifice.

5. God determines the fundamental Laws of Nature and causes them to be obeyed.

6. God can cause violations of physical laws[3] but does not appear to have done so. In chapter 8 we see that God can cause/modify events by using Quantum "tweaks." These "actions" of God do not violate Physical Law but could account for miracles and other unusal events.

7. God and His activities are independent of distances and coordinate systems.

8. God is aware at all times of all in the Cosmos[4] in infinite detail in the past, present and future. Figuratively God can be thought of as *simultaneously* viewing all parts of a complete infinite tape (We call it the Tape of Fate.) of everything in the Cosmos in all detail for all time

1.2 Hawking vs. God

Professor S. Hawking's last book[5] states his claim:

There is no God.

Steven Hawking

---

[2] In Islam God is viewed as a combination of spirit and matter.

[3] In principle God can violate Physics conservation laws and dynamics laws due to His Omnipotence.

[4] The Cosmos consists of the entirety of physical creation including masses, energies, quantum vacuum(s), in all universes.

[5] S. Hawking, *Brief Answers to Big Questions* (Bantam, London, 2018).

The basis of Hawking's opinion, as he states it, is that the laws of Physics need no "help" from God, working perfectly and being well wrought. He conceptualizes, without mathematical proof, that the universe sprang from a vacuum fluctuation and evolved from there according to Physical Law. Thus, no need for a God. However Hawking does not explain the origin of the Quantum vacuum or of Physical Laws. In the case of the standard Big Bang Theory there is nothing—no vacuum and no coordinates outside the point universe. Thus Hawking faces a quandary—nothing from which the universe can appear as a fluctuation. DeWitt, Unruh and other physicists have pointed out that space and spatial distance, require a "yardstick" to measure distances. Similarly time measurements require a "clock." Yardsticks and clocks require matter and/or energy. Hawking's nothingness (not even a quantum vacuum) has neither. Thus his concept is questionable.

A contrary point of view suggests God made the laws of Physics and causes their successful execution in such a way that His direct intervention is not needed. In addition, as we discuss in chapter 8, there is a Quantum escape valve that enables God to intervene in events in such a way as not to violate laws of Physics. Thus God is present but not in an "obvious" manner. As Einstein remarked,"The Lord is subtle." Hawking's concept may stand as a method followed by God, but neglects the deeper level of Reality "engineered" by God.

The mysteries of the Origin of Everything leads us to say:

There is God.

2. Analyzing the Nature of God and the Cosmos

2.1 Reaching the Fundamental: God and Cosmos

This study of God[6] and the Cosmos is predicated on the belief that Physics, at the most fundamental level, can lead to a scientific view of God and the Cosmos. This author developed a fundamental theory of Physics called The Unified SuperStandard Model[7] that derived Physics from a fundamental set of axioms in a manner analogous to Euclid's derivation of Geometry.

The basis of these axioms is an entity, called the Umoved Mover by many Philosophers and Theologians, that "introduces" dynamical motions (change) in the Cosmos. The requirements for dynamics led to the axioms of the Unified SuperStandard Model.[8]

In turn, the nature of the Unmoved Mover became of interest as well as the general properties of the Cosmos. This book addresses these questions. Its approach to the dynamics of the Unmoved Mover does not rely particularly on the Unified SuperStandard Model although that is where the questions originated. It can be viewed as based on any correct, deep, fundamental Theory of Everything. The features of the Unmoved Mover presented in Blaha (2018b) are suggestive of what many view as God. However identifying the Unmoved Mover with God requires a leap of faith that many would make while others would not.

---

[6] **We assume that there is but one God - monotheism.** Some religions are *polytheistic* with many gods. However almost all polytheistic religions assume that one primary god exists that begins Creation and generates a family of secondary gods. In that sense polytheistic religions are "disguised" monotheistic religions.

[7] See Blaha (2018a) which is based on a series of many books by the author starting in 1999.

[8] Blaha (2018b).

2.2 God in the Great Modern Religions

The Great Modern Religions: Buddhism, Christianity, Confucianism, Hinduism, Islam, Judaism, Shintoism, Zoroastrianism, and so on, have varying views of God. Nevertheless, there is a great deal of commonality. Most of their descriptions of God are based on religious views, revelations, philosophic generalities, and other inspiration.

In this book we will approach God and the Cosmos based on logic and scientific concepts. We see this approach as solid and scientifically convincing although many aspects of God, described in religious writings, go much further into topics (such as emotions and morality) that a scientific approach cannot explain.

2.3 A Scientific Approach: Fundamental Tools

Assuming that God exists and is the Unmoved Mover of Philosophy and Theology (at least in part) we now describe the tools which, we believe, enable us to understand aspects of God and the Cosmos, and to clarify conflicting concepts in the theologies of various religions.

2.3.1 Logic

The most important tool for the scientific understanding of any phenomena is Logic. We intend to apply Logic to the Divine, in a respectful way, to elucidate its features. (Some may remember that the consistency of Logic was questioned in the past based on apparent paradoxes and theorems such as Gödel's Theorem. In Blaha (2015a) we showed that these paradoxical results reflect a misunderstanding of the nature of logical statements. In particular, we pointed out that a statement is a form of function, stated in words and symbols, consisting of a predicate (the function) and a subject (the argument) that lies within the domain of the predicate (in the sense of function domains). Paradoxes and Gödel's Theorem use subjects (arguments) outside the domain of predicates. In mathematics functions have allowed domains of arguments. So also do statements have allowed domains of subjects for their predicates.

Thus Logic is unblemished and can be applied without concern to any phenomena.

2.3.2 Scientific Tools of Space and Time

The scientific concepts that will form the basis of of the tools for understanding God and the Cosmos are space and time. We will not use complex details such as the Theory of Relativity but will merely use space and time, logically considered, to develop a partial understanding of God and the Cosmos.

2.3.3 Knowing Scientifically

By knowing of God and the Cosmos scientifically the Reader will see that many of the points of religious discussions and dissensions will be clarified and resolved.

3. God In Itself

The understanding of the nature of God in the World's Religions varies. There are many facets of God that Religions address. In this chapter we will examine the nature of God in Itself from a scientific view with *no* Cosmos present. God in Itself! Naturally the aspects of God that we will consider, within this context, are limited. We cannot, for example, scientifically consider God's emotions or other topics frequently discussed in religious literature. However we will find that our considerations are not without interest.

3.1 In the Beginning There was No Beginning

Most religions and scientific theories assume a "beginning." However we shall see that the existence of a beginning naturally implies a "before time." In the case of all religions (primitive and modern) there is usually a primal God.[9] The God of all religions exists for all time[10] eliminating the need for a prior deity.

In the case of scientific theories, there is usually a beginning such as the Big Bang, or a primal emergent state (such as a quantum vacuum) of unspecified origin, or a theoretical framework that simply "is." Scientific theories are thus burdened by a gnawing "before the beginning" issue. Typically the issue is not considered or only lightly considered or put back to an earlier beginning.

In this book we have chosen to assume the infinite existence of God (in the past and future) removing the issue of "the Beginning."

---

[9] Noted by Mircea Eliade, *Patterns in Comparative Religion* (Sheed and Ward, New York, 1958).

[10] Some primitive religions have their primal god "disappear" or become "useless" in favor of newer gods.

3.2 Unmoved Mover

If *only* God (the Unmoved Mover) exists, without any Cosmos or other things, then God has no physical nature, has no size or extension, and *cannot change* since time and space do not exist except as part of the Cosmos. Then God exists as unchangeable (Unmoved) but not as a Mover in the absence of the Cosmos.

3.3 No Thought or Emotions Beyond Loneliness

If God cannot change, then God would not be able to have any sequences of thought or emotion. Thus God would be an unchanging entity that could not, for example, create a Cosmos.

With only existence in itself, God only would be capable of permanent loneliness[11] at best—not loneliness for any thing—but loneliness in itself. His "loneliness" is analogous to the loneliness that humans can feel. But it is not the same. Also God's purported loneliness should not be considered as directed solely towards Mankind but for all of Creation with its many species (intelligent and otherwise.).

3.4 What Do We Learn From These Considerations

Given the static nature of a God *alone*, God could not Create the Cosmos at some specific instant. For that would violate the above found constraints despite the assumption of a God with unlimited power and abilities.

3.5 The Cosmos has No Beginning and No End

We conclude that the Cosmos must always have been in existence. A lonely God with nothing else "present" cannot have ever existed. For then there would be no Creation of the Cosmos.

---

[11] Please remember that this is a hypothetical surmise IF there were no Cosmos. The existence of the Cosmos forever eliminates God's loneliness forever.

4. The Cosmos in Itself

4.1 What is the Cosmos?

We define the Cosmos to be all of Creation including all matter and energy in galaxies, our universe and any other universes that might exist.[12] (We called the space of all universes the Megaverse in earlier books.) Since the Cosmos has dynamical evolution, time(s) must be defined in all universes and the Megaverse (if it exists). And space must exist within, and between, universes for dynamics to take place. Perhaps the best way to view the Megaverse is by analogy with our universe. The Megaverse is analogous to our universe with its universes analogous to galaxies and the space between its universes analogous to the space between galaxies.

4.1.1 Reasons for Believing in Other Universes

In Blaha (2018a) we gave a number of experimental reasons[13] for believing in a space of universes based on astrophysical concepts that we reproduce here for the reader's convenience:

> At first glance it would seem impossible to produce evidence for the existence of other universes. However there are subtle means by which we can 'sense' experimentally 'nearby' universes should they exist. The mechanism would appear to be gravitational effects exerted on objects within our universe by unseen objects of enormous mass. Currently there appears to be three experimental suggestions of the existence of 'nearby' universes and one theoretical argument based on an influx of mass-energy from the Megaverse that may support an understanding of the expansion of our universe.
>
> **4.1.2 Great Attractors**
>
> One potential support is the discovery of the Great Attractor (at the center of the Laniakea Galaxy Supercluster), and the more massive Shapley Attractor (centered in the Shapley Supercluster)[14].

---

[12] A quantum vacuum is implicit in this definition of the Cosmos.

[13] Important theoretical reasons are also presented there.

These attractors contain massive numbers of galaxies and are drawing galaxies over a distance of millions of light years towards them.

If another universe(s) is 'near' our universe it could act as a 'gravitational magnet' and draw galaxies within our universe towards it to form one or more superclusters which could then act as attractors. Thus attractors might indirectly reveal the presence of other nearby universes—contrary to the expected large scale uniformity of the universe. The only other apparent source of superclusters is chance. Chance seems an unsatisfactory possibility in the present case.

4.1.3 Bright Bumps in Universe Sugesting Collision with Another Universe

A recent study[15] of the residual brightness of parts of the accessible universe found that bright patches appeared if a model of the CMB (Cosmic Microwave Background) with gases, stars and dust was 'subtracted' from the PLANCK map of the entire sky. After the subtraction one would expect only noise spread throughout the sky. However, bright patches were seen in a certain range of frequencies. These anomalies are thought to be a result of our universe colliding with another object – presumably another universe in the Megaverse.

4.1.4 Cold Spot in Universe Suggesting Collision with Another Universe

Another recent study[16] of a huge cold region of the universe spanning billions of light years revealed that this region is not a relatively empty region but rather is similar to in its distribution of galaxies to the rest of the universe. Previous the Cold Spot (an area where cosmic microwave background radiation – the leftover Big Bang radiation is weak – making it significantly colder (0.00015C colder) than the average temperature of the universe.)

An analysis of 7,000 galaxy redshifts using new high-resolution data has now shown that the Cold Spot is similar to the rest of the universe. The Durham University group suggested that the Cold Spot might have been caused by a collision between our universe and another Universe. They further suggested that there is only a 1 in 50 chance that it could explained by standard cosmology. could produce this feature

Thus we have another important piece of circumstantial evidence in favor of other universes and thus the Megaverse.

---

[14] Tully, R. Brent; Courtois, Helene; Hoffman, Yehuda; Pomarède, Daniel, "The Laniakea Supercluster of galaxies". Nature (4 September 2014). 513 (7516): 71–73; arXiv:1409.0880.

[15] Ranga-Ram Chary, arXiv.org:/1510.00126 (2015).

[16] T. Shanks et al, Durham University (Australia), Monthly Notices of the Royal Astronomical Society, 2016 .

4.2 Megaverse Energy-Matter Infusion into Our Universe

In chapter 14 of Blaha (2017c) we presented a model for an influx of mass-energy from the Megaverse to support the Bondi-Gold-Hoyle-Narlikar Steady State Cosmology, which was originally based on the 'continuous creation of mass-energy' by Hoyle and Narliker. This model explains why the value of Ω makes the universe close to flat. If this model is correct then we would have concrete support for a Megaverse with a low mass-energy density leaking mass-energy into our universe. *More generally, it suggests that universes are surfaces of high mass-energy density in a Megaverse of low mass-energy density – with a ratio of mass-energy densities of the other of 10^{30}.*

4.3 Conclusion

We conclude that data is beginning to emerge favoring multiple universes and a physical Megaverse in support of the theoretical justifications presented earlier.

There are also important theoretical arguments for believing in the Megaverse. See Blaha (2018a).

4.3.1 The Cosmos and Possible Non-Physical Additional Spaces: Heaven, Hell and So On

The physical Cosmos is briefly described above. A number of Religions suggest that other "spaces" of a non-physical nature exist such as Heaven, Hell, and so on. These "spaces" are considered in chapter 11.

4.4 How Did It Start or Did It Always Exist?

In the previous chapter we showed that the Cosmos must always have existed due to the nature of God. This conclusion leads to the following possibilities:

1. If the Cosmos consists only of our universe then our universe must have existed into the infinite past. The universe may have been subject to oscillations in size from a point (a Big Bang point) to some large size. Or it may have been a point

for an infinite amount of time and then "one day" it began expansion. Both possibilities have been considered by theoretical physicists.[17]

2. If the Cosmos is a Megaverse with any number (innumerable?) of universes within it, then universes can interact (collide), generate new universes, destroy universes, and so on. Then our universe may be one universe that came into existence at some remote time and persists.

In any case the Cosmos must have existed forever and will continue to exist forever into the future. The reason is simple: If the Cosmos should begin or end at some time then God would be in a static state before or after as describedearlier. If this happened we would have a God that is time-dependent contrary to our assumption of a God who exists independent of time. Time is, after all,an artifact (part) of the Cosmos and does not exist independent of the Cosmos.

The Cosmos has always existed and will exist forever.

4.5 How May God View the Cosmos?

In view of eternal nature of the Cosmos, we may rightly inquire of God's view of the Cosmos. Perhaps the best view that God might have of the Cosmos is that of an infinite tape (The Tape of Fate) recording everything in the Cosmos in infinite detail. God views the tape in its entirety, always, since he must know all. God does not need time travel since He/She exists with perfect knowledge of eternity always.

[17] Another possibility that has surfaced recently is that our universe is but one of an infinite succession of universes that persist from aeon to aeon. A signature of this succession of universes would be Hawking points that are shadowy remnants of past universes. See D. An, K. A. Meissner, R. Penrose, "Apparent Evidence for Hawking Points in the CMB Sky" arXiv:1808.01740 (2018) for a theoretical discussion. Suggestive new evidence from the BICEP 2 team for Hawking points is presented in D. An, K. A. Meissner, and P. Nurowski, Mon. Not. Roy. Astron. Soc 3251, **473** (2018).

4.6 Predestination

Given God's perfect knowledge of the past and future, one might think that *Predestination* follows. Predestination "removes" free will by making all events predetermined by the "inexorable will of God." A person does not have freedom of choice (free will) in this view but consciously or unconsciously follows God's will.

In chapter 8 we will consider Predestination and will show that God knows the past, present and future completely, and yet free will (choice) still exists in the Cosmos if the Cosmos is Quantum.

4.7 The Limitless Power of God Over the Cosmos

The limitless power of God is a true fact[18] but since the infinite past and future is fully known to God, God's power is seen at all times (past and future), by God, to have been exercised at specific points in the Cosmos' evolution.

God sees the Cosmos' Tape of Fate in its entirety at all times. All God's "acts" are known to God for "all time."

4.8 The Earth and the Cosmos

The earth is one very small part of the Cosmos. However in all religions the earth plays a central role. So we must consider the earth in view of the infinite nature of the Cosmos.

4.8.1 Earth Creation and Armageddon

Most religions specify a Beginning and Ending for earth. While the Cosmos exists forever, the creation of the planet earth occurred at a particular point in time, and will end at some particular time in the future. The end is sometimes called Armageddon. The "end" of the earth (whatever and whenever that is) does not end the Cosmos, which exists for all time past and future.

More generally astronomical bodies: other planets, stars, galaxies, and universes may begin and end but the Cosmos containing them continues.

---

[18] By our initial assumption of a limitless God.

4.8.2 Other Worlds: Other Beginnings and Ends

Countless other worlds exist in the Cosmos. They have their own beginnings and ends.

5. Physical Aspects of the "Creation" of the Cosmos

5.1 The Logic of the Laws of the Cosmos

The physical laws of the Cosmos, which Mankind has been researching for millennia, appear to be drivable from a set of axioms rather like the laws of geometry are derivable from five axioms. To logically derive the physical laws of Nature a certain natural path can be followed:

1. The requirements for Nature to exist as we know it must be specified. (Section 5.3)

2. From these requirements a consistent set of axioms must be specified. (Appendix A lists the axioms for our Unified SuperStandard Model—which is increasingly viewed as the only viable Theory of Everything.)

3. The theory must be derived from axioms. (Blaha (2018a) and (2018b)

4. Possibly? more fundamental sets of axioms, and consequent theories, must be considered.

Based on earlier chapters it must be realized that the Creation of the Cosmos is an event that did not happen as an event because the Cosmos has existed forever and will continue to exist forever. Thus Creation is a concept and not a physical (or spiritual) event at a point in time.

5.1 Was the Cosmos Created?

In chapters 2 and 3 we saw that the Cosmos must always have existed and must continue to exist forever. In this chapter we examine why the Cosmos has the form that it has by considering the fictitious case of an initial Creation of the Cosmos. We ask why[19] did God create the Cosmos in the manner in which he did?

5.2 God's Apparent Creation Rationale

The derivation of the Physical theory[20] of the Cosmos, as we know it, has certain fundamental prerequisites if one wishes to have dynamical physical processes, as we know them, to occur. Any attempt to create a universal physical theory must meet these prerequsites.

5.3 Some Fundamental Prerequisites for a Fundamental Physics Theory of the Cosmos

We can list some[21] fundamental prerequisites based on a general knowledge of the necessary nature of a fundamental theory of Physics.

1) A time variable must exist that may have various forms,

2) We wish to have a dynamical fundamental theory that evolves in time. Thus there must be a mechanism(s) that allow dynamical processes to exist that may, or may not, run in parallel.

3) Multiple parallel physical processes can execute.

4) There must be a space with a coordinate system(s), and a distance measure, within which processes can execute.

---

19 The Creation of the Cosmos was considered in Blaha (2018b).

20 Blaha (2018a) and (2018b) present a complete "Theory of Everything" for the Cosmos. The reader does not need to know the details of the theory to understand this chapter and following chapters.

21 Blaha (2018b) contains a more complete list of axioms.

5) There must be wave-particles upon which dynamical processes execute.[22]

6) The theory must be Quantum.

7) Creation should opt for Vitamorphic[23] universes that support life in some form. Recent studies have shown that evolution favors the development of increasingly intelligent life. Thus the ultimate appearance of intelligent life at places within universes appears to be natural, making the *Anthropic Principle* an evolutionary consequence[24] of the *Vitamorphic Principle.*

These prerequisites would seem to be necessary and "sufficient" for the specification of a fundamental Physics theory of the Cosmos.

5.4 God Theory and the Unified SuperStandard Model

As we will see God Theory has many important consequences. One very important consequence is our Unified SuperStandard Model which follows from the above considerations and the resulting axioms of Appendix A. The closeness of our Unified SuperStandard Model to God Theory has led some to suggest The Unified SuperStandard Model should be called the God Theory of Everything. We feel that a separation of the two theories is more advisable since each theory stands on its own merits although there is a clear possible connection.

---

[22] Those who believe God is the Word would probably also require that the number of fundamental wave-particles should be finite (although languages with an infinite number of characters can be constructed.) In our Theory of Everything (The Unified SuperStandard Model) there are 192 fermions (spin ½ particles) and 192 vector bosons (spin 1 particles) plus spin 2 gravitons. Thus the symbols of this theory's language is finite.

[23] The *Vitamorphic Principle* states that universes should support some form of life realizing that there are many varieties of life and borderline forms of life. A 'tight' definition of life has not been satisfactorily constructed. There are many borderline entities that may or may not be called life. We take 'Vitamorphic' to mean 'life enabling' in English. Vitamorphism is not a concept without meaning—a universe (Megaverse) consisting of only inert matter without energy present would be non-Vitamorphic. The Anthropic Principle, briefly put, states that intelligent human-like life should exist. We pronounce "Vitamorphic" in Latin style as "Veeta-morphic."

[24] One can well wonder whether the emergence and dominance of Mankind has eliminated the possibility of the emergence of other intelligent species on earth from the many semi-intelligent species that exist now and in the past.

6. God's Composite Nature

6.1 God and the Cosmos

In earlier chapters we saw that God (the Unmoved Mover) requires the Cosmos to have a dynamic aspect. The Unmoved Mover specifies the nature of the Cosmos through the considerations of chapter 4 which lead to the axioms presented in Appendix A. The derivation of The Theory of Everything in Blaha (2018a) and (2018b) gives the Standard Model of Elementary Particles plus much more. The Unmoved Mover determines and causes the dynamics (the "Movement") of the evolving Cosmos. As we saw earlier the Cosmos exists forever so the Creation of the Cosmos by the Unmoved Mover, although it is done by God, is "before time" since time is an artifact of the Cosmos. Time did not exist before Creation. Thus Creation does not happen at some instant but really exists forever as an "implicit" part of God (with the Unmoved Mover).

6.2 Is the Cosmos Part of God?

Or does God permeate the Cosmos? If the Cosmos is a distinct part of a Godhead composed of the Unmoved Mover, the Cosmos, and perhaps additional parts then we must ask how the Cosmos partakes of God-like features. If we regard the Cosmos as merely matter and energy, as Physicists view it, then there is no Godliness in the Cosmos. So an enhanced theory of the Cosmos would be required, such as that of Leibniz,[25] where particles of matter and energy have a divine "spark." An enhanced theory of the Cosmos would put the Cosmos on a God-like footing and unite It with the Unmoved Mover. See Table 6.1 (below) for a comparison of features of God and the Cosmos. The fact that they both exist forever is a strong argument for a God-like

---

[25] Leibniz viewed all particles of matter as containing a devine spark – his *monad* theory. See Rescher (1967).

Cosmos. Spinoza suggested a similar pantheistic view of the Cosmos. Karl Krause coined a name for a version of this view, which he called *panentheism*.

A panentheistic view of the Cosmos distinguishes the Cosmos from the Unmoved Mover. So we must consider the possibility that the Godhead has at least two parts: the Unmoved Mover and the "panentheistic" Cosmos that acquires "Godhood" in its particles of matter and energy—perhaps through divine sparks (monads?) or a similar mechanism.

The godliness of the Godhead then is due to the godliness of Its parts. A primary feature of godliness is its infinity of existence. The Unmoved Mover and the Cosmos both have an infinite existence.

6.3 God's Relation to the Cosmos – The Connection

We have distinguished the Unmoved Mover from the Cosmos with both partaking of the Godhead. The Unmoved Mover is connected to the Cosmos by causing natural laws to be obeyed throughout the Cosmos. It is also possible that the Unmoved Mover, by exerting Its will and unlimited power, may cause events (interventions) to take place within the Cosmos that we might view as miracles or at least strange phenomena. (Chapter 7 describes a mechanism for God to act in the Cosmos to achieve Its will without violating the Physical laws of the Unified SuperStandard Model.)

The *Connection* between the Unmoved Mover and the Cosmos could be viewed as simply a "transmission" between them. It might also be viewed as an entity with God-like properties. From previous chapters we see the Connection must be eternal—without beginning or end. The Connection must partake of the divinity of the Unmoved Mover and the Cosmos to achieve dynamical control of the Cosmos by the Unmoved Mover, and to support intervention by the Unmoved Mover in the Cosmos. The method by which it achieves these goals is in the interaction between the Unmoved Mover and the Cosmos.

If the Cosmos has sparks of divinity, then the Connection—connecting both divine parts—must have a divine aspect. Its "infinitesimal" parts must also have a spark of the divine.[26]

Thus we arrive at *a triune Godhead consisting of the Unmoved Mover, the Cosmos, and the Connection between them.* Table 6.1 compares the features of the parts.[27] Fig. 6.1 diagrams the interrelations of the parts in the Godhead.

Is there one God? Yes, according to our assumption and ensuing discussion. We merely provide a logical separation of God into parts.

In Appendix B we will discuss the nature of the Connection in some detail within the framework of our Unified SuperStandard Model. Lay readers may choose to skip this somewhat technical chapter since it does not play a role in the discussions in succeeding chapters.

---

[26] Perhaps as Leibniz-like monads. See Appendix B for a "particulate" form of Connection. The particles of the Connection would have a divine spark just as the particles of the Cosmos.

[27] One cannot say that the three parts of the Godhead are as separated as our analytical discussion suggests. They may well be inseparable. Also, the possibility of other parts is not precluded.

ENTITY	NATURE	LIFETIME	ROLE
Unmoved Mover	Spirit	Forever	Creates and Causes Dynamics
Cosmos	Spirit/Material	Forever	Scene of dynamic Activity
Connection	Spirit	Forever	Connects God, as Unmoved Mover, to the Cosmos, and intervenes in Cosmos events

Table 6.1. The entities of existence. The Cosmos can be viewed as spirit if all forces between its parts are zero. In reality there are forces and so the Cosmos is "material.".

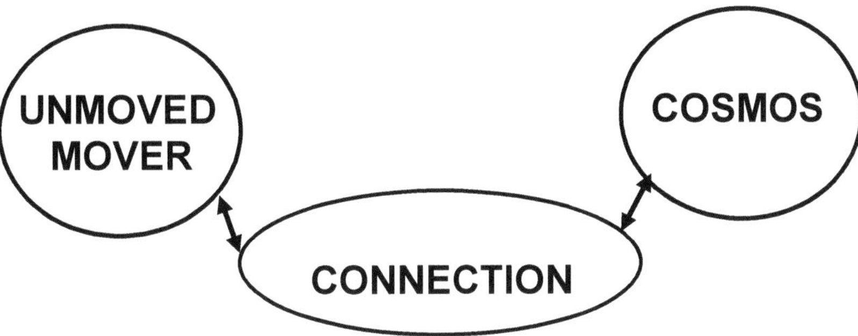

Figure 6.2. Relations between the three logical parts of the Godhead. The lines between the parts signify the "communications" channels between the parts..

Figure 6.3 Completely interspersed God with all parts combined. Yahweh as interspersed God.

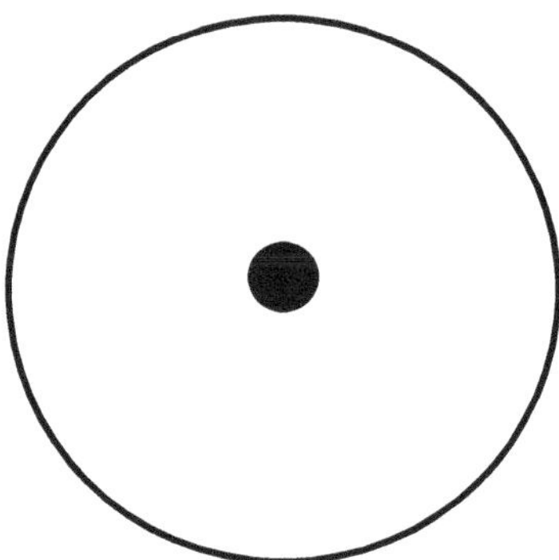

Figure 6.4. The monad —ancient religious/philosophical symbol representing the divine.

Amalgamations are possible among the three parts as seen below.

6.4 Christianity

6.4.1 Christ as combined from Cosmos and Connection

Jesus Christ could be viewed as a combination of the Cosmos (He had a material nature.) and the Connection. (He was viewed as directly connected to God.) His references to the Father might be interpreted as references to the Unmoved Mover.

6.4.1 Holy Ghost/Spirit

The Holy Ghost/Holy Spirit could be viwed as a composite of the Connection and the Unmoved Mover. The Holy Spirit would then be able to "sense" and instigate motion.

6.5 Judaism

Judaism has one God composed of all three parts described above. However it does differentiate between a High God who stands above it all, and a Living God that is more involved with Mankind. One can view the High God as the Unmoved Mover and the Living God as composed of the Cosmos and the Connection parts.

6.6 Islamic God *tawhid*

The Islamic God, called *tawhid*, is strictly monotheistic—inherently one. It is both material (part of the Cosmos) and spiritual (part of the Unmoved Moder and Connection).

6.7 Buddha

The Buddha would seem to be composed of the Cosmos only.

6.8 Lord Krishna

Lord Krishna appears to be a composite of the Cosmos and the Unmoved Mover.

7. Predestination, Free Will and Quantum Theory

Fixed Fate, free will, foreknowledge absolute.
J. Milton, *Paradise Lost*, Book ii, line 560

Predestination is a troubling concept that is accepted in some religions and rejected by others. It states that all events happen through the design of God and that free will does not truly exist—free will is an illusion.

In this chapter we will suggest that Quantum Theory enables free will to exist, enables God to intervene in the Cosmos without violating Physical Laws, and yet enables God to be all-knowing of events past and future in all detail with "foreknowledge absolute" through the Tape of Fate.

7.1 God's Tape of Fate of the Cosmos and Predestination

Earlier we suggested the view that God, in effect, has an infinite tape containing all aspects of the Cosmos from the remote past to the remote future. His foreknowledge indicates that he is fully aware of the entire contents of the tape everlastingly in the past and future.[28]

God's "foreknowledge absolute" is the predestination to which many religions refer. It appears to eliminate the possibility of arbitrary intervention by God into Cosmic events at selected points in a manner not present in the tape. Yet God's intervention does occur according to all religious thought and any intervention by God must appear in the Tape of Fate since it is a faithful record of eternity.

---

[28] Time travel, which appears to be possible in principle, can be accommodated within the Tape of Fate as simply a flattening of the tape segments for a time travel trip to one composite tape segment—a multiplexed tape segment.

God cannot arbitrarily and randomly intervene in Cosmic events because God's Physical Laws cannot be violated—superficially contradicting God's assumed limitless power. A moment's thought shows that all of God's interventions at various times in the "infinite life" of the Cosmos must have existed as a reality forever—from the infinite past to the infinite future of the Cosmos. Thus we have the issue of intervention without violation of Physical Laws.

7.2 The Need for a Quantum Cosmos

In Blaha (2018a) we suggested that Quantum Theory was the simplest way to ensure that matter and energy were both made of discrete particles.

We now consider another, perhaps deeper, justification for Quantum Theory. While Quantum Theory has many facets, one factet of great importance in our view, is that it introduces chance into physical processes. When an event takes place, such as the collision of two particles, there can be varying results of the collision. Each possible result has a certain probability of happening—just as flipping a coin has a probability of "coming up" heads and a probability of "coming up" tails.

7.2.1 God's Intervention in the Cosmos

The introduction of chance in physical events opens a "new" possibility for God's intervention in Cosmic events. Without chance God's intervention would be strictly limited by Physical Law (which He established absolutely) making "miracles" very limited, and in most cases impossible.

With chance in physical events, it becomes possible for God to "tweak" an event quantum mechanically to make a certain result happen. This result can then cause a series of further events to happen possibly with additional Quantum tweaks and so on.

The result is a cascading set of events caused by Quantum tweaks consistent with Quantum probability, and Physical Law—a chain reaction of events that can generate a miracle or even change history. One remembers here the lament of Richard III of England, "My kingdom for a horse." (We will not comment on the chain of events that would have put a horse within Richard's grasp.)

7.2.2 Quantum Source of Free Will

Free will is usually viewed from the aspect of a person's mental state. However, free will has several forms. Some forms relate to the person's perceived situation with free will exercised to maximize the person's benefit and/or views. This form involves a significant part of the person's consciousness.

Another form of free will is chance decisions. A good example of this form is spot decisions as to where to place chips on a roulette table. This type of decision can be based on guessing and may reflect a chance event in a person's mind. Free will based on chance miniscule events in a person's mind can be the result of cascading Quantum tweaks.

Thus a person can have free will without God's intervention. But God can also intervene by making Quantum choices of outcomes in a person's neurons.

God can thus intervene in the Cosmos to implement change, guide free will, and execute miracles through Quantum effects.

7.3 Quantum Observer Problem

Having brought in Quantum Theory to support intervention by God we must now consider an important Quantum Theory problem that is resolved by the existence of God.

The problem is the need for a Quantum Observer to view an event and observe which of the possible results actually occurs in reality. A famous example is Schrödinger's Cat. A cat is placed in a box with a radioactive element that decays after a "random" time. The setup in the box causes the cat to die when the radioactive element decays. The problem is: After x minutes is the cat alive or dead? The answer can only be found if the box is opened by an observer. Before that point in time the cat is in an unknown state with the reality of its life in doubt.

Thus reality becomes an issue of observation. Some have suggested that complete knowledge of the entire element-cat-box apparatus as a quantum state would resolve the issue. But that is unlikely because the composite system is quantum and subject to chance as well.

One could extend the apparatus state to the entire universe. But that would still be quantum.

So the tenure of the cat's lifetime remains uncertain forever. A sad situation.

The situation of Schrödinger's Cat applies throughout the Cosmos. It appears that reality is an ever present issue for the Cosmos.

7.4 God as the Ultimate Quantum Observer

The only clear-cut solution to the reality problem is God—the Ultimate Quantum Observer.[29] God need only look at His "tape" to see the results of all Quantum events. Thus God gives reality to the Cosmos.

7.5 Events Without Observers

The question raised in some religions: does an acorn make a sound when it falls to the ground if no one is present to hear the sound, is also resolved. God, the Unmoved Mover, is the omniscient Observer in all quantum and non-quantum events. It makes reality real whether or not a human observer is present.

7.6 God Knows All at All Times

All eternity is predestined since all events are known to God simultaneously at all times. Yet Quantum tweaks make it possible for God to make events happen without violating Physical Laws (that He/She established). *All* events are recorded on the Tape of Fate *forever* from the "Beginning" (which is not truly a beginning) to the end of eternity (which is not truly an end).

---

[29] Recently generalizations of the Schrödinger's Cat "experiment" have been considered in which an observer is placed in the box. Then it appears that if two observers, outside the box, open the box they will find different observations making a quantum paradox. This controversial result has been the source of much discussion..Again, our choice of God as the Ultimate Quantum Observer eliminates the paradox. See D. Frauchiger and R. Renner, arXiv:1710.05033v1 (2017) and arXiv:1604.07422v1 (2016) for detailed discussions of the paradox.

8. God Theory Results

8.1 God's Nature from a Scientific Perspective

This work began by extending the possibility raised by the Unified SuperStandard Model in Blaha (2018b) to assuming that the entity we previously called the Unmoved Mover was in fact God. Then with that assumption, and the presumed features of the Godhead, we proceeded to apply Physical thought and Logic to obtain a theory of God's nature from a scientific perspective.

We did not consider aspects of God that dominate theological discussions: Its mercy, Its Kindness, Its Love, Its relation to Good and Evil, and so on. These topics do not appear to be susceptible to Scientific analysis.

Nevertheless we obtained a view of God with noteworthy features that is consistent with much theological thought in most major religions. Our findings support notions of God that are prevalent in many religions. But they have a solid sciuentific/logical basis. Theological discussions are often based on principles that are founded in religious belief. A scientific basis with the primary assumption of one God and the secondary reality of the existence of the Cosmos has the ring of a deeper, more convincing Truth.

8.2 A Scientific View of God

Our major findings are:

1) The part of God called the Unmoved Mover needs the Cosmos.

2) The Cosmos exists forever in the past and the future. It is divine just as the Unmoved Mover. Together they are combined in God.

3) The Unmoved Mover and the Cosmos are 'joined" by a part called the Connection which exists forever and is divine as well.

4) The Connection implements the dynamics of Physical Laws in the Cosmos and performs any intervention required by the Unmoved Mover.

5) The Godhead consists of at least three divine parts: the Unmoved Mover, the Cosmos, and the Connection between them. Together the parts functionally form a triune God.

6) The Cosmos and Connection parts of God have a God-like nature that is represented in the Cosmos within the dynamics of the Unified SuperStandard Model or a similar Theory of Everything.

7) The Godliness present in the Cosmos, and the Connection, resides in a divine "spark" within the particles[30] of matter and energy within them—a form of panentheism.

8) The apparent contradiction between Predestination and Free Will is resolved by Quantum Theory.

8.3 Conclusion

We have developed a scientific analysis of God that joins naturally with our physical Theory of Everything: The Unified SuperStandard Model. As a result we have a chain of logic from an ultimate being, a divine Euclid, to a derivation of the form of Physical Reality as we know it, and additional features that remain to be found experimentally.

The similarity of our conclusions with the general form of modern major religions is encouraging.

---

[30] The divine spark resides within the Qubes and Qubas in particles and energy in our Unified SuperStandard Model.

Extension of God Theory to Mankind

9. God's view of Mankind

What is Man that God should be mindful of him? Astronomy, Physics and Astrophysics teach us that we are a small species on a minor planet in a very large universe that may be one of many universes. That being so, then God's Tape of Fate must be very filled with all the happenings of all the universe(s) of the Cosmos. And yet some religions say God is mindful of the flight of each sparrow.

So we are caught in the dilemma of our smallness in the vastness of God's Cosmos. Even so we can see that a number of points can be made that might reflect God's view of Mankind. (We note that the implicit spirit of chapters 1 – 8 was of a God focused on Mankind. But his focus must be on all creatures everywhere.)

We will determine as much as possible of God's view of Mankind by considering the state of Mankind under the assumption that God designed and set in motion the evolution of Mankind. What we are, and might be, must be viewed as the result of God's will. Some of the more important aspects of God's view of Mankind (on earth) determined from this ssumption are:

1. Mankind contains sparks of the divine (as do the animals and plants of earth.)

2. While life and living are of great importance to people, they may not be of much importance to God. It appears most religions have transitions after death that make death of less (or no) importance to God. For each of us has a place prepared for us by God. If one considers the 20th Century then we see a massive increase in the number of deaths due to war, disease and starvation as Sorokin (1941) points out. The 20th Century was the greatest "killing time" for Mankind. The increase in death might be an indication of God's indifference to death in favor of God's other "priorities." In line with these

thoughts, we note the English Book of Common Prayer states, "Death is the Great Victory." We note also that Socrates, among the "wisest" of Mankind, had a gathering of friends before his death (by a hemlock drink) and argued that death was not the end but the beginning of a new stage in the life of a soul. Socrates makes the telling point in his farewell address that we are all here to serve God and that God does not wish us to depart early, and not fulfill our service, but rather to complete our service by a natural death (or a death sanctioned by society as was the case for Socrates.) Thus God is against suicide.

3. Pain and suffering are of great importance to individuals. But these feelings are electromagnetic sensations Physically. In a certain sense they can be viewed as irrelevant to God. (Some religious groups such as Buddhists espouse this view. "Pain is an illusion.")

4. Good and Bad are relative terms that depend on present circumstances, and on future circumstances in some cases. What may be considered Good now may be viewed as being Bad in future. We see this often in politics. Also practices viewed as Good by one culture may be viewed as Bad by another culture. An outstanding example of this sort is the practice of the Carthaginians to sacrifice their first born males to their gods—a repugnant practice to the Romans and almost all of Mankind at present.

5. Bad individuals and practices may serve the Evolution of Mankind. We note the evils (murder, rape, and genocide) of the Spanish and English conquest of the Americas led to improved societies in most peoples' point of view: the United States, independent modern Hispanic countries, and so on. It should also be noted that in all non-European continents the leading wave of colonization was often mostly peopled by criminals, cutthroats, and fortune seekers motivated by Greed and Lust. Sadly Greed and Lust still seem the primary motivation for Mankind. See chapter 10 for a more detailed discussion of Evolution.

6. Item 4 above leads us to consider the punishment that we might face for being Bad (Hell and so on). If Bad is subject to differing views, then can a WISE AND JUST God banish people to Hell. It seems that punishment after death is questionable although almost universally believed. Considering the sources of Badness: genetic abnormalities and/or bad parental/societal treatment, it is difficult to believe God would punish people for Badness after death. Badness is a matter of circumstance. Mankind is relieved of blame for Badness in this light. Those who feel this idea destroys the motivation for religion should consider the universal hope for a wise and forgiving God. God should forgive those whose (God given) path in life leads them to Badness.

7. Before death, it seems just to punish Badness as a preventive measure for the benefit of society by imprisonment, execution, or other means. The author has felt for some time that Hell also exists on Earth for the Bad. Hell after death may, or may not, exist, although motives of hatred or revenge are often satisfied by belief in Hell after death. Hell on earth may happen for the Good as well (see Job). We hope it is due to God's greater plan.

8. God may prefer to let people expire into nothingness, or to begin fresh new lives through reincarnation (if it exists.) Heaven and Hell may be for the living—not the dead.

9. The life and death of a person might be irrelevant to God. Not from indifference but because it does not greatly affect God's "grand scheme" of Everything.

10. Prayer and sacrifice may influence God's plan for individuals: saving people from death or giving them a peaceful, painless death.

11. God can see that each of us is shaped by genetics, environment, and family social status to follow a God-chosen, high-walled path through life with the possibility of free will at times along the path. God's infinite power makes it possible for each of us to be so guided (as well as other beings in the universe(s).)

12. God views all beings as His/Her children subject to the evolution to a higher destiny.

Events of History (especially of recent history) suggest God does not conform to Mankind's view of the sacredness of human life. The evolution of Mankind from hunter-gatherers in caves to the present suggests God has a long term positive goal for Mankind paved with its ongoing woe, pain and suffering.

10. Good and Evil, and Darwinian Natural Selection

The two primary issues faced by Mankind with respect to its origin and progress are 1) Was Mankind directly created by God (Creationism) or did Mankind evolve through evolutionary mechanisms from "lower" species? and 2) Does "Survival of the Fittest" when applied to Mankind necessitate Evil: cruelty, murder, war, and so on? In this chapter we address these issues.

10.1 Origin of Life on Earth

The earth appears to be a not unusual locale for life to begin and evolve. We have found that life on earth begins with small creatures (viruses) and evolves to the large and varied life forms presently found (and that existed in the past.)

There appear to be reasons for the evolution of life rather than by direct creation of life by God. Direct creation of life would be a violation of God's Physical Laws. God does not violate Physical Laws but God can cause Quantum Tweaks to engineer interventions in physical phenomena.

10.1.1 Creationism

Creationism requires God's Physical Laws to be directly violated. There is no evidence that God's Laws have been violated. Therefore Creationism does not appear to be correct.

10.1.2 Evolution

Thus we see that the only mechanism for life to appear/evolve/change is through evolution not direct creation. When considering the original forms of life that appear through chemistry, we find the first forms appear to be viruses or RNA. On earth all life evolves from that beginning.

There is an important reason for life to begin in the "small." Life depends on energy.[31] Small life forms can obtain energy from local (small) physical environments. They can then evolve to larger life forms (that consume energy from larger sources) eventually reaching the large sizes of creatures found today and in the time of the dinosaurs and before—all through the application of Physical Laws.

In discussions of creationism vs. evolution the traditional basis of creationist claims is biblical. We suggest that the strict requirement of God's Physical Laws makes evolution from ultra-small organisms generated chemically the true choice of God.

Having justified evolution we now turn to the issue of the mechanism for evolution. We find that Darwin's theory of evolution through "Survival of the Fittest" supplemented by random genetic mutations appears to explain the evolution of life on earth within the framework of God's immutable Physical Laws.

Since the above discussion applies to other planets similar (or somewhat similar) to earth we believe Darwin's theory of evolution applies universally under suitable physical conditions.

10.2 Darwin's Survival of the Fittest

Darwinian evolution states that species evolve on earth through a mechanism that can be briefly described as "Survival of the Fittest" combined with chance genetic mutations. This view is based on variations in the population of each species, as well as the possibility of mutations, that cause a "favored" part of a species to more readily thrive within an environment. Thus the "less fit" part of a species gradually dies off leaving the most fit to live and further evolve.

The mechanism, fierce natural selection, for the enhanced prospects of a favored segment of a species' population leads eventually to their dominance, and the decline

---

[31] See Feinberg (1980) and Blaha (2010). Feinberg (1980) describes a fantastic variety of possible life forms in all sorts of environments from stars to huge gaseous planets to earth size planets to planetoids. All life forms require energy for their existence. Blaha (2010) shows that the rise and fall of civilizations is determined by the availability of energy.

(and perhaps extinction) of the less favored part of the species. Species use this mechanism to evolve.

10.3 Mutations

The "Survival of the Fittest" mechanism serves to cull species selecting their most viable parts to survive. It is known that the evolution of species also happens through spontaneous mutations appearing in the populations of species. A successful mutation in a species can lead to a "gradual" change in the species as the mutated individuals grow to dominate the species through Survival of the Fittest.

10.4 Good and Evil, and Survival of the Fittest

The muted (usually unstated) aspect of Survival of the Fittest mechanism is the fierce, often violent, struggles to achieve mastery by the favored part of a species. In the case of animals (and plants) these struggles are not viewed as conflicts between Good and Evil. They are simply natural phenomena.

In the case of Mankind there appears to be two phases to the social struggle. In the phase that dominated through most of Human history the struggles were mostly for territory, wealth, and "gods."

In the second phase, which appears to have primarily begun in the 19th century due to the increased literacy of the general population, the struugles have become struggles over ideas, economic systems, freedom, and the form of government. Good and Evil now come into play. Some ideologies are "Good." Some are "Evil". Thus we get Great Wars with each side claiming to be the Good side.

On the personal level individuals are Good or Evil according to the norms of their society and religion. Here we find that the struggle for wealth and riches, and the good things that come with them, leads people to choose a side explicitly or implicitly. The mushrooming of the struggle which often happens in depressed times, can lead to changes in the overall direction of a society. To some extent we see that happening in present day America where the struggle for wealth has increased the level of greed, crime, and violence.

10.5 Ascent of Mankind through Conflict

What are we to make of the present day struggles on personal and social levels. In both cases it appears that changes are being effected that will influence the eventual state of Mankind.

Can we say that God has arranged events to eventually bring about a greater Good? Or can we say that the random events that occur are without meaning as far as good and evil are concerned.

An instructive example to consider is the case of ants—the other dominant animals on earth.[32] Ants, like Mankind, are the only war-like creatures. They make war for territory and slaves.

It seems that violence and war, which Mankind views as Evil, may be a mechanism for Darwinian Survival of the Fittest. Thus the differentiation between Good and Bad is obscured by the ultimate goal of the advancement of Mankind.

10.6 God and Social Darwinian Selection

Then our view of God as favoring a totally peaceful world without crime may be mistaken. Perhaps Evils such as war are necessary to promote the "spiritual" growth of Mankind. Otherwise Mankind may simply exist as vegetative animals with no purpose or progress.

10.7 Mankind's Impact on Darwinian Survival of the Fittest

Mankind has begun to modify Darwinian Survival of Fittest from what it was before approximately 1900. Prior to 1900 there was much less pollution, much less debilitating/deadly chemicals in the soil and atmosphere, much more poverty without social remedies such as good, cheap medical treatment, much lower Medical knowledge, much more childbirth deaths. Death and short life spans were the "norm." Since 1900 we have seen major advances in Medicine, major social service increases, and so on. We have also seen more people surviving with genetic and other birth defects, and seen much more pollution of water, land and air.

---

[32] Ants make up 15 – 25 % of terrestrial animal biomass. Far more than humans. See Schultz, T. R., Proc. Nat. Acad. Sci. US, **97** (26), 14028 (2000).

The cumulative results of the advances and declines in the human condition is a growing decline in the genetic quality of the human race. People are living, and reproducing, with lower quality genetics. Darwin's Survival of the Fittest is being contravened by modern medicine, environmental pollution, and progressive social policies.

The long term question becomes: Will Mankind progress in the light of these new circumstances? One can hope the answer is "yes" because modern research in genetics and other areas might mitigate the effects of genetic degradation that we see at present.

10.8 Darwinism on Alien Worlds

The plethora of alien worlds upon which life in various forms could develop suggests that the Darwinian mechanism of Survival of the Fittest and the random genetic mutations to which all genetic material seems susceptible are likely to be prevalent in the universe(s). Thus we must be "prepared" for aliens that have gone through Darwinian evolution. *An alien history based on a Darwinian evolution would suggest aliens were acquainted with competition and warfare.* Thus they may be similar to Mankind in this regard. Approach with care!

We can hope that aliens will be amiable. We can hope that a common ground of understanding will exist. Blaha (2010) describes the possible progress that prolonged contact with aliens civilizations might engender. The time scales for rapprochement with alien civilizations ranges from hundreds to thousands of years depending on the relative levels of civilization of ourselves and the aliens.

11. Spiritual Spaces: Heaven, Hell, Purgatory, …

Various religions have spiritual "spaces" for people after they die. These "spaces" are pictured in a variety of human-like ways in paintings and literature. A physical point of view would suggest a different picture.

Since the people that go to Heaven, Hell, Purgatory, and similar "spaces" with other names in various religions, are there as immaterial souls, there is no need for physical spatial distance in them as we know it.

So we will not place these spaces in the Cosmos but view them as points in the mind of God with whatever features and purposes they serve. There is no other reasonable Physical statements we can make about them. Whether these places also contain the spirits of aliens cannot be stated with any degree of certainty.

12. Created Spirits: Souls, Angels, Demons, Spirits of Nature

All religions postulate the existence of spirits with a variety of features. These spirits were created by God. They appear in a variety of types that we will now consider. We will also contrast spirits with Dark Matter.

12.1 Souls

Souls are created by God. Their noteworthy feature is that they are given individually to creatures. Depending upon one's religion they are given to Mankind, animals, plants, and occasionally material objects such as statures or rocks.

When souls are given is a matter of dispute, which Physics cannot answer. They do not appear to be perceptible to physical investigation although some individuals claim to be able to sense them.

12.2 Angels

Angels are spirits created by God that exist as entities. They are immaterial. But they can influence matter if they so wish. They seem to have free will.

12.3 Demons

Demons are bad angels in common thought.

12.4 Spirits of Nature

Spirits of Nature are spirits associated with things of this world: rocks, springs, rivers, oceans, and animals. They are imperceptible but are capable of influencing people and material objects.

12.5 Ghosts

Ghosts are the remnant of the souls of humans after they die. Ghosts may or may not have natural effects apprehensible to Physical investigation.

12.6 Spirits vs. Dark Matter

Dark Matter is thought to permeate the universe. However it has not been found in the laboratory. It has the remarkable feature of interpenetrating normal matter. Both can coincide at the same points in space. The reason is simply that Dark Matter has minimal or no interaction with normal matter. Thus they cannot affect each other and can interpenetrate.

Spirits have somewhat similar properties according to religions. Spirits can interpenetrate matter. Spirits need not influence matter but can appear as apparitions in the space occupied by normal matter. Normal matter does not affect spirits except in special circumstances.

Are spirits made of Dark Matter? We believe not, because Dark Matter is influenced by gravity while spirits are not generally. Also spirits can assume a visible form while Dark Matter cannot.

There is a similarity. But that can only encourage us to believe that God can create spirits just like God can create Dark Matter.

13. God Theory's Related to the Theory of The Unified SuperStandard Model

The God Theory presented in this edition and the prior edition was born in a study of the axioms of the Unified SuperStandard Model of Elementary Particles developed by the author. God Theory can be viewed as the source of the Unified SuperStandard Model. On the other hand, the Unified SuperStandard Model can be viewed as an independent theory that stands on its own merits.

We indicate the relation of God Theory to the Unified SuperStandard Model and its other consequences in the below diagram.

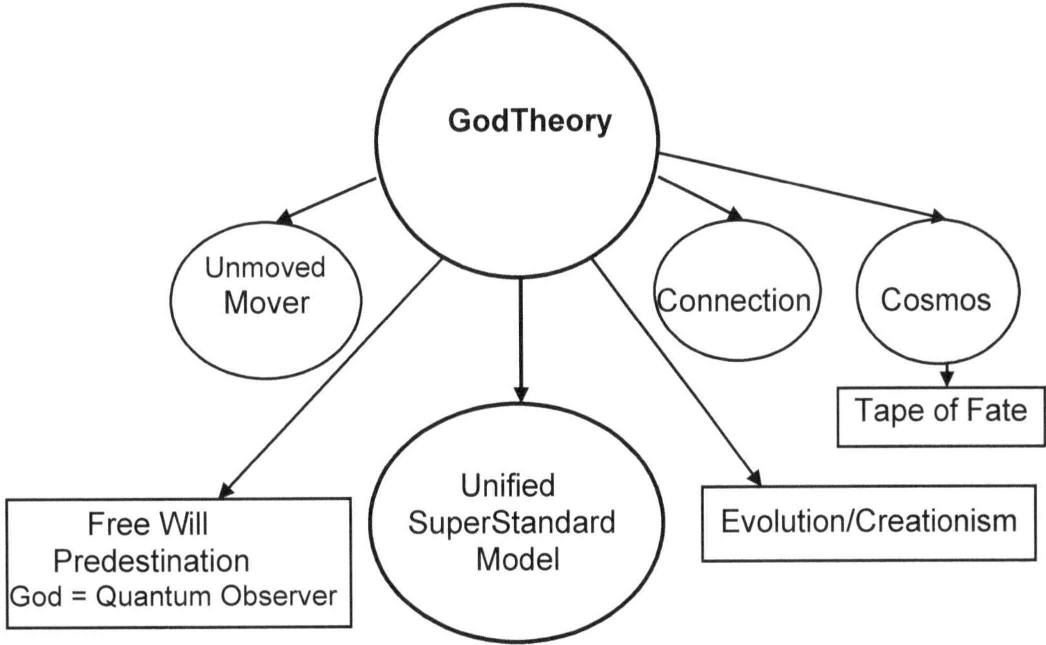

Appendix A. Enhanced Form of Unified SuperStandard Model Axioms

For the Reader's convenience we reproduce chapter 3 of Blaha (2018b) in this Appendix.

A.1 Underlying Basis of SuperStandard Axioms

In this chapter we present a revised set[33] of 'primitive' terms and axioms for our theory. A comparison of this new set of axioms with those provided in the Book will show that they are equivalent but add a few new axioms. They are also more simply stated, have fewer overlaps between axions, and cleanly lead to the Book's theory of elementary particles.

The goal of the Book and this volume is to derive the Unified SuperStandard Model in the manner of Euclid with a clear connection between the steps of the derivation just as Euclid developed geometry from a progression of theorems.

A.2 Primitive Terms and Axioms

Primitive terms can be as simple as those of Euclid or they can be more complex. The level of simplicity depends on the nature of the theory and the Physical Laws that emerge from it. In the case at hand, a fundamental unified theory, the constructs that emerge in the construction of the theory are mathematically complex. Consequently, the choice of primitive terms and axioms may be expected to be mathematically complex as well, unless one wishes to expand the primitive terms into a more detailed, term by term description in simpler, more basic primitives. We will not pursue that alternative here since the terms that we use are 'self-explanatory' to the

---

[33] The Book is Blaha (2018b). The Book presents axioms in chapter 0.

Elementary Particle Physics theorist knowledgable about quantum field theory and particle symmetries.

A.3 Mathematics and Conceptual Prerequisites

Due to the complexity of the Theory we have chosen to specify mathematics prerequisites and use them in the derivation rather than devoting parts of the derivation to mathematical preliminaries. Therefore we use complex variable theory, Riemannian coordinates, group theory, classical and Quantum Logic, functionals, Chomsky-like computational languages, and so on without bringing in unnecessary supporting details from them.

We also assume certain physical concepts such as distance, quantum features, second quantization, covariance under a group transformation, and spatial curvature.

The list of axioms uses some of these prerequisite concepts treating them as primitive terms for the derivation.

A.4 Primitive Terms for the Unified SuperStandard Model

The somewhat revised set of primitive terms of the theory are:

Qubits
Qubes
Qubas
Core
Grammar
Terminal and Nonterminal Symbols
Production Rules
Speed of Light
Spatial Dimensions
Space and Time Coordinates
Covariance under group transformations
Asynchronous processes
Parallel Processes
Reference Frame
Complex Lorentz Group
General Coordinate Transformations
Gravity

Universe
Particle Masses
Fermions
Bosons
Particle States
Particle Rest State
Particle Momenta
Spin
Canonical Quantization
Quantum Process
Quantum Entanglement
Second Quantization
Quantum Field Theory
Quantum States
Asymptotic Particle States
Internal Symmetries
Coupling Constants
Discrete Symmetries
Yang-Mills Local Gauge Theory
Functionals
Functional space

In choosing these primitives, we understand that they generally embody a significant theoretic description or body of knowledge. We do not include names used in the mapping to reality (such as quark) in the list of primitives since the mapping to reality is a separate issue in our view.

A.5 Revised Axiom Set for the Unified SuperStandard Model

The somewhat revised set of axioms that we list below is supplemented by the Decision Axioms of Appendix C.1.3 of the Book. The 'new' physical axioms are

PARTICLE AXIOMS

1. All matter and energy is composed of particles.
2. Each fundamental particle has a physico-logic structure within it that we designate its core.

3. Particles form an alphabet with a finite number of characters and combine in ways specified by the quantum probabilistic production rules of a quantum computational grammar.[34]
4. A core is a particle functional that combines with a free field fourier coordinate expansion in an inner product to produce a free second quantized particle field.
5. There is a 4-dimensional space of particle functionals, called *particle functional space*,with the distance measure eq. A.1 specifying the transformation group of particle functionals.
6. Particle functional space consists of a single point.
7. The core of a fermion functional is called a *qube*. Fundamental bosons have a core consisting of a boson functional called a *quba*.
8. Qubes have a a bare mass. Qubas have zero mass.

SPACE AXIOMS

9. The dimensions of a coordinate space-time are determined by the number of fundamental[35] interactions, and the requirement that all parallel processes, with parts perhaps separated by distances, can occur synchronously.
10. Spatial coordinates are inherently complex-valued.
11. Space has one complex-valued component that plays the role of time. Physical phenomena dynamically evolve based on the time variable.
12. The infinitesimal distance ds between two space-time points is given by

$$ds^2 = dt^2 - d\mathbf{x}^2 \quad \text{(A.1)}$$

where $d\mathbf{x}$ is a vector of the spatial coordinates. Transformations between coordinate systems preserve the value of ds and define a transformation group. (The Complex Lorentz Group)

13. Physically acceptable reference frames have real-valued coordinates. These coordinates can be obtained by group transformations from complex-valued coordinate systems. Physical space-time measurements are made in a real-valued coordinate system.
14. The speed of light is the same in all reference frames.
15. Free fundamental leptons must have a real-valued energy.
16. Gravity may cause space-time to be curved. (Complex General Coordinate transformations[36])

---

[34] See Blaha (2005b).

[35] Interactions that would exist in the absence of fermion particles.

[36] If the metric tensor of space-time is analogous to one of the metric tensors of the superfluid phases of ^{3}He, then space-time might have several metric tensors in 'various regions.' If the space-time metric tensor is analogous to the ^{3}He-B superfluid phase metric tensor, which has an effective gravity with a complex metric tensor, the space-time metric tensor would be the familiar one of General Relativity. However if the space-time metric tensor is analogous to the metric tensor of superfluid ^{3}He-A, which exists at higher pressure and temperature, then the space-time metric tensor might be similar to the Penrose twistor theory metric tensor. In this case the corresponding General Relativity may have a twistor-like metric tensor: perhaps in the early universe, and/or inside black holes, and/or in small

DYNAMICS AXIOMS

17. The complete theory has a lagrangian formulation. If the lagrangian is truncated to quadratic form (interactions set to zero) then symmetries appear that are the source of particle symmeytry groups that persist with broken symmetry after interactions are reintroduced. The lagrangian specifies a set of production rules of a type 0 Chomsky language generalized to include production rules for the generation of all strings of symbols (particles) from any strings of symbols (including the *head symbol.*)[37]
18. The lagrangian of the theory must be invariant under coordinate system transformations.
19. Dynamical particle equations must be covariant under group transformations.
20. All interactions have a local Yang-Mills gauge theory formulation.
21. The vector bosons, and the interactions among them, are determined by terms in complete lagrangian, some of whose parts are obtained from the Riemann-Christoffel Curvature Tensor.

QUANTIZATION AXIOMS

22. All fields must be canonically quantized.
23. Fermion and Boson vacua can be defined that are valid in all coordinate systems.
24. The number of particles in an asymptotic state of any given type is invariant in all reference frames.
25. Quantum processes starting in an initial quantum state, with parts separated by a distance after a time, can have the parts synchronously change each other instantaneously. (Quantum Entanglement)

---

universes with higher pressure and temperature than our universe. We will assume the conventional metric for Complex Special and General Relativity.

[37] Chapter 8 of Blaha (2018b) discusses computational languages for particles in detail.

Appendix B. Possible Mechanism of the Connection and Cosmos Parts of God

This chapter describes a possible mechanism for the Connection based on our Unified SuperStandard Model.[38,39] The fermion (spin ½) fundamental fermions in the Unified SuperStandard Model are depicted in Fig. B.1. The possible newly found particles have a ? mark next to them. We base our placement in the fourth generation on a heavier new neutrino mass, and a heavier (than an electron) electron-like particle mass.

B.1 Fermion Spectrum of the Unified SuperStandard Model

This section describes the "Periodic Table" of fermions (spin ½ fundamental particles like electrons, neutrinos, quarks and so on). It is analogous to the Periodic Table of Elements in Chemistry.

[38] Much of the material appeared in Blaha (2018a) and (2018b).

[39] The week of September 17, 2018 saw public announcements of a possible fourth generation neutrino seen at the Super-Kamiokande giant particle detector. If so, it would be a potential confirmation of the four fermion generations predicted by our Unified SuperStandard Model. Since then new particles have also been found that passed through the earth without generating an interaction shower. They may be second layer, charged leptons (heavier siblings of the electron.) See the paper D. B. Fox et al, arXiv:astro-ph.HE 1809.09615 (2018). The fact that these particles traverse earth without an interaction shower indicates they do not have known Standard Model interactions. Thus they are most likely members of a higher fermion layer. See Fig. B.1.

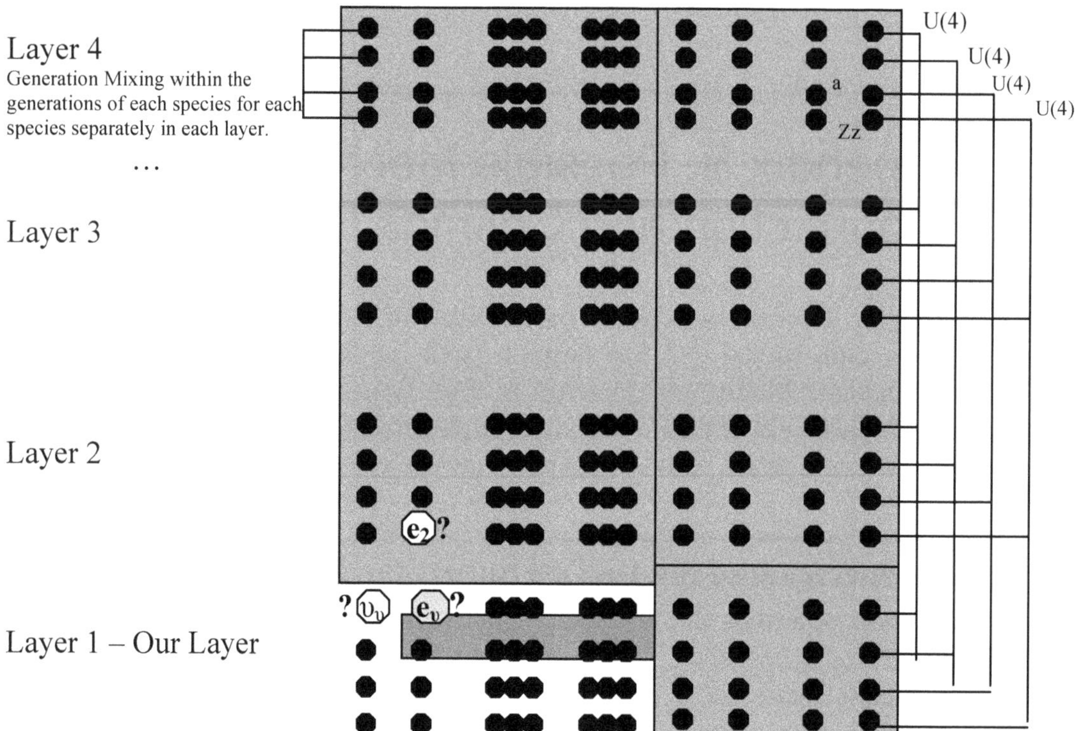

Figure B.1. Partial example of pattern of particle transformations of the Generation group and of the Layer groups.. Dark parts of the periodic table are not yet found. Light parts are the known fermions..The "dot" labeled $\mathbf{υ_υ}$ followed by a ? mark represents a possible new heavy neutrino where υ represents a lower case Greek Ypsilon. The other "dot" labeled $\mathbf{e_2}$ followed by a ? mark represents a possible new heavy electron-like particle *of the second fermion layer*. This particle went through the earth without generating an interaction shower. A third "dot" represents a proposed charged lepton $e_υ$ that is the "partner" of $ν_υ$. The lines on the left side show an example of the Generation mixing within one species. The Generation mixing applies to each species in each layer. The lines on the right side show the Layer mixing generation by generation.among all four layers for each generation individually. See Blaha (2018a) for a detailed discussion.

We choose to provisionally identify the e_2 particle as a second layer electron-like particle because it traversed the earth without creating an interaction shower. The interaction between particles in different layers can be expected to be ultraweak in the Unified SuperStandard Model. (The subscript $_2$ indicates a second layer particle.)

The first layer neutrinos are then e, μ, τ, and the proposed υ – a fourth generation charged lepton.

The new particles are encouraging support for the Unified SuperStandard Model.

B.2 Joining of Connection and Cosmos

The "union" of the Connection with the Cosmos is implemented by associating *two* quantum fields with every particle of matter and energy.[40] In Blaha (2018a) and (2018b) we implemented this formulation of the SuperStandard Model for major technical reasons.

Based on our preceding discussions here, we now attribute a greater significance to the two field formulation. We identify one of the fields, in each pair of fields for a particle, as a Connection field that supports the roles of the Connection: 1) as forcing reality to conform to the Laws of Physics as set up by the Unmoved Mover, and 2) as implementing possible "Divine Intervention" by the Unmoved Mover. This field is typically labeled with a "1". The other field, which we label with the index "2", is a Cosmos field that generates the physical dynamics of Reality manipulating matter and energy. The dynamics equations are the result of the Connection fields in a lagrangian formulation.

In this book we have assumed that all particles of matter and energy have a spark of divinity within them that taken together makes both the Cosmos and Connection divine. Thus the fields of both type "1" and type "2" have a divine spark

[40] Both boson and fermion particles.

within them (when their particle relation is considered) by assumption—an assumption required in order to have a divine Cosmos and a divine Connection.

B.3 Technical Reasons for "Two Fields per Particle" Formulation

The Unified SuperStandard Model, and earlier work, pioneered the use of a quantum field theoretic formalism that associated two second quantized fields with every elementary particle. The two field formalism was also used to develop a generalization of Quantum Mechanics that united classical fields with quantum fields. (This formalism enabled a "continuous" transformation (rotation) to be made between strictly quantum fields and "corresponding" strictly classical fields.

In the Unified SuperStandard Model we used the two second quantized fields formalism in four situations:

1. The formalism was applied to Higgs boson fields to obtain a formulation that cleanly separated the vacuum expectation value of a Higgs particle's field from its second quantized part.

2. The formalism was applied to higher derivative dynamic parts to obtain a canonical lagrangian formulation via the Ostrogradski Bootstrap mechanism. The higher derivative sector generated quark confinement through a manifest linear potential, and a gravitational potential that had three forms depending on distance in a manner similar to MOND gravity. But without modifying fundamental Newtonian law.

3. The formalism resolves the well-known problem of ambiguities between second quantization in different reference frames. In the 1970's the author showed that the formalism could resolve second quantization ambiguities using Bogoliubov transformations. Second quantization then becomes "covariant" under changes of coordinate systems.

4. The two field formalism, if used in Quantum Mechanics, supports continuous transformations between quantum mechanics and classical mechanics, and

allows for pseudo-quantum mechanics intermediate between quantum mechanics and classical mechanics. Such intermediate mechanics may appear in the "gray" zone that one sometimes sees in atomic theory.

B.4 Divine Cosmos and Divine Connection

The Connection is god-like through sparks of godliness within the fields of type "1" that are like the *qubes* and *qubas* of matter and energy in the universe (and the Megaverse) in our Unified SuperStandard Model.

The Unified SuperStandard Model specifies the dynamics of the divine Cosmos through the control on type "2" fields exerted by the type "1" fields of the Connection. Both Connection and Cosmos have Qubes and Qubas containing divine sparks.

The Unmoved Mover uses the Connection to constrain the Cosmos to obey Physical Laws and to possibly intervene in the Cosmos.

B.5 Unmoved Mover, Connection and Cosmos

Having linked the Cosmos and the Connection we now see the Unmoved Mover part of God to be the *unltimate source* (Origin) of Everything thus bringing our Unified Standard Model to completion.

REFERENCES

Blaha, S., 1998, *Cosmos and Consciousness 2nd Edition* (Pingree-Hill Publishing, Auburn, NH, 2003).

______, 2014c, *All the Megaverse! II Between Megaverse Universes: Quantum Entanglement Explained by the Megaverse Coherent Baryonic Radiation Devices – PHASERs Neutron Star Megaverse Slingshot Dynamics Spiritual and UFO Events, and the Megaverse Microscopic Entry into the Megaverse* (Blaha Research, Auburn, NH, 2014).

______, 2014c, *All the Megaverse! II Between Megaverse Universes: Quantum Entanglement Explained by the Megaverse Coherent Baryonic Radiation Devices – PHASERs Neutron Star Megaverse Slingshot Dynamics Spiritual and UFO Events, and the Megaverse Microscopic Entry into the Megaverse* (Blaha Research, Auburn, NH, 2014).

______, 2010, *SuperCivilizations: Civilizations as Superorganisms* (McMann-Fisher Publishing, Auburn, NH, 2010).

______, 2015b, *PHYSICS IS LOGIC Part II: The Theory of Everything, The Megaverse Theory of Everything, U(4)⊗U(4) Grand Unified Theory (GUT), Inertial Mass = Gravitational Mass, Unified Extended Standard Model and a New Complex General Relativity with Higgs Particles, Generation Group Higgs Particles* (Blaha Research, Auburn, NH, 2015).

______, 2016e, *MoND: Unification of the Strong Interactions and Gravitation II, Quark Confinement Linked to Large-Scale Gravity, Physics is Logic IX* (Blaha Research, Auburn, NH, 2016).

______, 2016f, *CQ Mechanics: A Unification of Quantum & Classical Mechanics, Quantum/Semi-Classical Entanglement, Quantum/Classical Path Integrals, Quantum/Classical Chaos* (Blaha Research, Auburn, NH, 2016).

______, 2016g, *GEMS: Unified Gravity, ElectroMagnetic and Strong Interactions: Manifest Quark Confinement, A Solution for the Proton Spin Puzzle, Modified Gravity on the Galactic Scale* (Pingree Hill Publishing, Auburn, NH, 2016).

______, 2016h, *Unification of the Seven Boson Interactions based on the Riemann-Christoffel Curvature Tensor* (Pingree Hill Publishing, Auburn, NH, 2016).

______, 2017c, *Megaverse: The Universe of Universes* (Pingree Hill Publishing, Auburn, NH, 2017).

______, 2017f, *The Unified SuperStandard Model in Our Universe and the Megaverse: Quarks, ... ,* (Pingree Hill Publishing, Auburn, NH, 2017).

______, 2018a, *The Unified SuperStandard Model and the Megaverse SECOND EDITION A Deeper Theory based on a New Particle Functional Space that Explicates Quantum Entanglement Spookiness (Volume 1)* (Pingree Hill Publishing, Auburn, NH, 2018).

______, 2018b, *Cosmos Creation: The Unified SuperStandard Model, Volume 2, SECOND EDITION* (Pingree Hill Publishing, Auburn, NH, 2018).

______, 2018c, *God Theory (*Pingree Hill Publishing, Auburn, NH, 2018).

Feinberg, G. and Shapiro, R., 1980, *Life Beyond Earth: The Intelligent Earthling's Guide to Extraterrestrial Life* (Morrow, New York, 1980).

Rescher, N., 1967, *The Philosophy of Leibniz* (Prentice-Hall, Englewood Cliffs, NJ, 1967).

Sorokin, Pitirim, 1941, *Social and Cultural Dynamics* (Porter Sargent Publishers, Boston, MA, 1941).

INDEX

About the Author

Stephen Blaha is a well known Physicist and Man of Letters with interests in Science, Society and civilization, the Arts, and Technology. He had an Alfred P. Sloan Foundation scholarship in college. He received his Ph.D. in Physics from Rockefeller University. He has served on the faculties of several major universities. He was also a Member of the Technical Staff at Bell Laboratories, a manager at the Boston Globe Newspaper, a Director at Wang Laboratories, and President of Blaha Software Inc and of Janus Associates Inc. (NH).

Among other achievements he was a co-discoverer of the "r potential" for heavy quark binding developing the first (and still the only demonstrable) non-abelian gauge theory with an "r" potential; first suggested the existence of topological structures in superfluid He-3; first proposed Yang-Mills theories would appear in condensed matter phenomena with non-scalar order parameters; first developed a grammar-based formalism for quantum computers and applied it to elementary particle theories; first developed a new form of quantum field theory without divergences (thus solving a major 60 year old

problem that enabled a unified theory of the Standard Model and Quantum Gravity without divergences to be developed); first developed a formulation of complex General Relativity based on analytic continuation from real space-time; first developed a generalized non-homogeneous Robertson-Walker metric that enabled a quantum theory of the Big Bang to be developed without singularities at t = 0; first generalized Cauchy's theorem and Gauss' theorem to complex, curved multi-dimensional spaces; received Honorable Mention in the Gravity Research Foundation Essay Competition in 1978; first developed a physically acceptable theory of faster-than-light particles; first derived a composition of extrema method in the Calculus of Variations; first quantitatively suggested that inflationary periods in the history of the universe were not needed; first proved Gödel's Theorem implies Nature must be quantum; provided a new alternative to the Higgs Mechanism, and Higgs particles, to generate masses; first showed how to resolve logical paradoxes including Gödel's Undecidability Theorem by developing Operator Logic and Quantum Operator Logic; first developed a quantitative harmonic oscillator-like model of the life cycle, and interactions, of civilizations; first showed how equations describing superorganisms also apply to civilizations. A recent book shows his theory applies successfully to the past 14 years of history and to *new* archaeological data on Andean and Mayan civilizations as well as Early Anatolian and Egyptian civilizations.

He first developed an axiomatic derivation of the form of The Standard Model from geometry – space-time properties – The Unified SuperStandard Model. It unifies all the known forces of Nature. It also has a Dark Matter sector that includes a Dark ElectroWeak sector with Dark doublets and Dark gauge interactions. It uses quantum coordinates to remove infinities that crop up in most interacting quantum field theories and additionally to remove the infinities that appear in the Big Bang and generate inflationary growth of the universe. It shows gravity has a MOND-like form without sacrificing Newton's Laws. It relates the interactions of the MOND-like sector of gravity with the r-potential of Quark Confinement. The axioms of the theory lead to the question of their origin. We suggest in the preceding edition of this book it can be attributed to an entity with God-like properties. We explore these properties and show they predict that the Cosmos exists forever although individual universes (or incarnations of our universe) "come and go." The Unified SuperStandard Model has many other important parts described in the Second Edition of *The Unified Superstandard Model* and expanded in subsequent volumes.

Blaha has had a major impact on a succession of elementary particle theories: his Ph.D. thesis (1970), and papers, showed that quantum field theory calculations to all orders in ladder approximations could not give scaling deep inelastic electron-nucleon scattering. He later showed the eigenvalue equation for the fine structure constant α in Johnson-Baker-Willey QED had a zero at $\alpha = 1$ not 1/137 by solving the Schwinger-Dyson equations to all orders in an approximation that agreed with exact results to 4th order in α thus ending interest in this theory. In 1979 at Prof. Ken Johnson's (MIT) suggestion he calculated the proton-neutron mass difference in the MIT bag model and found the result had the wrong sign reducing interest in the bag model. These results all appear in Physical Review papers. In the 2000's he repeatedly pointed out the shortcomings of SuperString theory and showed that The Standard Model's form could be derived from space-time geometry by an extension of Lorentz transformations to faster than light transformations. This deeper space-time basis greatly increases the possibility that it is part of THE fundamental theory.Recently, Blaha showed that the Weak interactions differed significantly from the Strong, electromagnetic and gravitation interactions in important respects while these interactions had similar features, and suggested that ElectroWeak theory, which is essentially a glued union of the Weak interactions and Electromagnetism, possibly modulo unknown Higgs particle features, be replaced by a unified theory of the other interactions combined with a stand-alone Weak interaction theory. Blaha also showed that, if Charmonium calculations are taken seriously, the Strong interaction coupling constant is only a factor of five larger than the electromagnetic coupling constant, and thus Strong interaction perturbation theory would make sense and yield physically meaningful results.

In graduate school (1965-71) he wrote substantial papers in elementary particles and group theory: The Inelastic E- P Structure Functions in a Gluon Model. Phys. Lett. B40:501-502,1972; Deep-Inelastic E-P Structure Functions In A Ladder Model With Spin 1/2 Nucleons, Phys.Rev. D3:510-523,1971; Continuum Contributions To The Pion Radius, Phys. Rev. 178:2167-2169,1969; Character Analysis of U(N) and SU(N), J. Math. Phys. 10, 2156 (1969); and The Calculation of the Irreducible Characters of the Symmetric Group in Terms of the Compound Characters, (Published as Blaha's Lemma in D. E. Knuth's book: *The Art of Computer Programming Vols. 1 – 4*).

In the early 1980's Blaha was also a pioneer in the development of UNIX for financial, scientific and Internet applications: benchmarked UNIX versions showing that block size was critical for UNIX performance, developing financial modeling software, starting database benchmarking comparison studies, developing Internet-like UNIX networking (1982) and developing a hybrid shell programming technique (1982) that was a precursor to the PERL programming language. He was also the manager of the AT&T ten-year future products development database. His work helped lead to commercial UNIX on computers such as Sun Micros, IBM AIX minis, and Apple computers.

In the 1980's he pioneered the development of PC Desktop Publishing on laser printers. and was nominated for three "Awards for Technical Excellence" in 1987 by PC Magazine for PC software products that he designed and developed.

Recently he has developed a theory of Megaverses – actual universes of which our universe is one – with quantum particle-like properties based on the Wheeler-DeWitt equation of Quantum Gravity. He has developed a theory of a baryonic force, which had been conjectured many years ago, and estimated the strength of the force based on discrepancies in measurements of the gravitational constant G. This force, operative in D-dimensinal space, can be used to escape from our universe in "uniships" which are the equivalent of the faster-than-light starships proposed in the author's earlier books. Thus travel to other universes, as well as to other stars is possible.

Blaha also considered the complexified Wheeler-DeWitt equation and showed that its limitation to real-valued coordinates and metrics generated a Cosmological Constant in the Einstein equations.

The author has also recently written a series of books on the serious problems of the United States and their solution as well as a book on the decline of Mankind that will follow from current social and genetic trends in Mankind.

In the past twelve years Dr. Blaha has written over 40 books on a wide range of topics. Some recent major works are: *From Asynchronous Logic to The Standard Model to Superflight to the Stars, All the Universe!, SuperCivilizations: Civilizations as Superorganisms, America's Future: an Islamic Surge, ISIS, al Qaeda, World Epidemics, Ukraine, Russia-China Pact, US Leadership Crisis,The Rises and Falls of Man – Destiny – 3000 AD: New Support for a Superorganism MACRO-THEORY of CIVILIZATIONS From CURRENT WORLD TRENDS and NEW Peruvian, Pre-Mayan, Mayan, Anatolian, and Early Egyptian Data, with a Projection to 3000 AD,* and *Mankind in Decline: Genetic Disasters, Human-Animal Hybrids, Overpopulation, Pollution, Global Warming, Food and Water Shortages, Desertification, Poverty, Rising Violence, Genocide, Epidemics, Wars, Leadership Failure.*

He has taught approximately 4,000 students in undergraduate, graduate, and postgraduate corporate education courses primarily in major universities, and large companies and government agencies.

www.ingramcontent.com/pod-product-compliance
Ingram Content Group UK Ltd.
Pitfield, Milton Keynes, MK11 3LW, UK
UKHW052228270726
14060UKWH00004B/659